If not for You, Lord,
I could not do this life.

GALE ALVAREZ

WORD & SPIRIT
PUBLISHING

The print ready cover graphics and interior formatting were provided by Word & Spirit Publishing. Creative direction provided by Julio Vitolo.

Cover image used by permission of Shutterstock.

Back cover author photo taken by Albaner C. Eugene Jr.

Scripture quotations marked (KJV) are taken from the King James Version Bible. Public Domain.

Scripture quotations marked (NKJV) are taken from the New King James Version®. Copyright © 1982 by Thomas Nelson. Used with permission. All rights reserved.

Scripture quotations marked (ESV) are taken from The Holy Bible, English Standard Version® (ESV®), Copyright © 2001 by Crossway, a publishing ministry of Good News Publishers. Used with permission. All rights reserved.

Scripture quotations marked (NIV) are taken from The Holy Bible, New International Version®, NIV®. Copyright © 1973, 1978, 1984, 2011 by Biblica, Inc.® Used by permission of Zondervan. All rights reserved worldwide. www.zondervan.com. The NIV and New International Version are trademarks registered in the United States Patent and Trademark Office by Biblica, Inc. TM

Scripture quotations marked (NASB) are taken from the New American Standard Bible®, Copyright © 1960, 1962, 1963, 1968, 1971, 1972, 1973, 1975, 1977, 1995 by The Lockman Foundation. Used with permission. (www.Lockman.org)

Scripture quotations marked (NLT) are taken from the Holy Bible, New Living Translation, Copyright © 1996, 2004, 2015 by Tyndale House Foundation. Used by permission of Tyndale House Publishers, Inc., Carol Stream, Illinois 60188. All rights reserved.

Scripture quotations marked (AMP) are taken from the Amplified® Bible, Copyright © 2015 by The Lockman Foundation. Used with permission. (www.Lockman.org.) All rights reserved.

Scripture quotations marked (BSB) are taken from the Berean Study Bible. The Holy Bible, Berean Study Bible, BSB. Copyright ©2016, 2020 by Bible Hub. Used with permission. All rights reserved worldwide.

Scripture quotations marked MEV (Modern English Version)

ISBN: 978-1-735788-05-0

Published by Word and Spirit Publishing
P.O. Box 701403, Tulsa Oklahoma 74170
Wordandspiritpublishing.com

In connection with Gale Alvarez, Love of Jesus Ministries, Inc., 448 Highland Avenue, Orange, NJ 07050

GALEALVAREZ.COM

CONTENTS

I would have lost heart, unless I had believed
That I would see the goodness of the LORD
In the land of the living.
Psalm 27:13 NKJV

— �֟ —

Therefore I will look unto the LORD;
I will wait for the God of my salvation;
my God will hear me.
Micah 7:7 KJV

Introduction

The book that you hold in your hand was born out of a trying time in my life. I felt like I was being squeezed, abused, and misunderstood. I sat at my desk with tears streaming down my face, and I began to write. Writing has always been a healthy expression for me to get rid of the turmoil, and truly, it does bring relief and release on the inside, the part that no one sees but God. As I wrote the words, "If Not for You, Lord," my thoughts went to the God of all creation in whom nothing is too difficult. Life brings many seasons, and if I know anything for sure, it is that I could not make it through a day, a night, or a season without my Lord. "If Not for You, Lord," is now my focused writing, and it is unending because He is unending in what He has done, is doing, and what He is yet to do in a surrendered life. Moreover, the God of all creation is unending in who He is and all He is to me.

As a response to my "If Not for You, Lord," thoughts, I began to write my gratitude to God for His unending, irreplaceable place in my life. I believe that gratitude will turn the tide of despair into God's faith, into His hope that does not disappoint, and into His unfailing love. We have so much to be thankful for, and surely, we have way more going for us than we have coming against us. It is my prayer that you would allow God to water you as you read and meditate on the magnitude of who God is, on all the "If Not for You" moments, and on the life He has bestowed upon you. And then may we all lift our hearts and hands together with joy-filled expectation and declare, "Thank You, Lord."

"So let us know—let us press on to know the LORD.
As surely as the sun rises, He will appear;
He will come to us like the rain,
like the spring showers that water the earth."

Hosea 6:3 BSB

Author's Prayer and Reflection

Dear Lord,

I pray that every reader of this book will find their home in You. Home, an open door, a place of safety, and a room of understanding even when we ourselves feel so misunderstood. Home, a place of acceptance, a refuge, a hug from the inside out, and a space of love poured out. Home, a hearing ear, a room full of light and full of You, Lord, available to all who will come into Your presence. May we come to a full understanding that IF NOT FOR YOU we will never find what we are looking for or what we are in need of in this life. May the knowledge of You bring us to the One who has all the answers and to You in whom we can place our trust. Thank You, Lord, for being HOME to me. To every reader, I say, WELCOME HOME!

The eternal God is your refuge,
and underneath are the everlasting arms.

Deuteronomy 33:27 NIV

— ✻ —

What a fellowship, what a joy divine,
Leaning on the everlasting arms;
What a blessedness, what a peace is mine,
Leaning on the everlasting arms.

Leaning, leaning,
Safe and secure from all alarms;
Leaning, leaning,
Leaning on the everlasting arms.

Leaning on the Everlasting Arms
Authors: Elisha A. Hoffman & Anthony J. Showalter
PUBLIC DOMAIN

If not for You, Lord,
 I could not do this life
If not for You, Lord,
 I would stay lost and never found
If not for You, Lord,
 my heart would stay broken and never be
 made whole
If not for You, Lord,
 my cries would go unheard
If not for You, Lord,
 in the darkness there would be no light
If not for You, Lord,
 I would not know You, the light of the world
 who always illuminates my darkness
If not for You, Lord,
 I would never win any of life's fights
If not for You, Lord, If not for You

— �֍ —

**Come to Me, all you who are weary and burdened,
and I will give you rest.**
Matthew 11:28 BSB

Thank You, Lord,
> for helping me in my time of need

Thank You, Lord,
> for being a voice in the silence

Thank You, Lord,
> for being a safe place of refuge

Thank You, Lord,
> for interpreting and bottling up my tears

Thank You, Lord,
> for grace sufficient in each day, for grace
> sufficient in every season

Thank You, Lord,
> for being the way, the truth,
> and the life

Thank You, Lord,
> that those who sow with tears will reap
> with songs of joy

Thank You, Lord, Thank You, Lord

I will praise the name of God with a song,
And will magnify Him with thanksgiving.

Psalm 69:30 NKJV

If not for You, Lord,
    there would be no signs or wonders
If not for You, Lord,
    there would be no grace for this space
If not for You, Lord,
    I would only survive and not thrive
    in life's seasons
If not for You, Lord,
    there would be no living water for my thirst
If not for You, Lord,
    the well would run dry
If not for You, Lord,
    I would faint in my journey
If not for You, Lord,
    I would never have found love
If not for You, Lord, If not for You

And God *is* able to make all grace abound toward you,
that you, always having all sufficiency in all *things*,
may have an abundance for every good work.

2 Corinthians 9:8 NKJV

Thank You, Lord,
   that You do miracles every day
Thank You, Lord,
   for leaving the 99 to go find the one
Thank You, Lord,
   for life in abundance
Thank You, Lord,
   that Your mercy never runs out
Thank You, Lord,
   that Your Spirit revives me
Thank You, Lord,
   that with You I pass all of life's tests
Thank You, Lord,
   for being the constant in my life
Thank You, Lord, Thank You, Lord

— ✚ —

The steadfast love of the Lord never ceases;
his mercies never come to an end; they are
new every morning; great is your faithfulness.
"The Lord is my portion," says my soul,
"therefore I will hope in him."

Lamentations 3:22–24 ESV

If not for You, Lord,
    the sun would not shine
If not for You, Lord,
    the moon would not set
If not for You, Lord,
    the seasons would not change
If not for You, Lord,
    peace and calmness would be out of reach
If not for You, Lord,
    I would have no one to teach me the way
If not for You, Lord,
    I would not know the power of stay
If not for You, Lord,
    I would not know life's way
If not for You, Lord, If not for You

The heavens declare the glory of God;
the skies proclaim the work of His hands.

Psalm 19:1 BSB

Thank You, Lord,
> for being the light in my days

Thank You, Lord,
> for being my bright in my night

Thank You, Lord,
> for being the Alpha and the Omega
> for being my calm in every storm

Thank You, Lord,
> for being constant in every season
> for always being my reason

Thank You, Lord,
> for the freedom of worship

Thank You, Lord,
> for the vocabulary of prayer
> for daily being fresh air

Thank You, Lord, Thank You, Lord

In Him was life, and the life was the Light of mankind.

John 1:4 NASB

If not for You, Lord,

    I would not know the truth.

If not for You, Lord,

    I would not know "that anyone who belongs
    to Christ has become a new person. The
    old life is gone; a new life has begun!"
    (2 Corinthians 5:17 NLT)

If not for You, Lord,

    I would not know the new birth

If not for You, Lord,

    I would not know my worth

If not for You, Lord,

    I would not know how to dress

If not for You, Lord,

    my life would be a mess

If not for You, Lord,

    I would never pass any of life's tests

If not for You, Lord, If not for You

— �֍ —

Jesus said to him, "I am the way, the truth, and the life.
No one comes to the Father except through Me.

John 14:6 NKJV

Thank You, Lord,
  for the hope of Heaven above
Thank You, Lord,
  that you teach me your ways
Thank You, Lord,
  for teaching me to thrive in each season
Thank You, Lord,
  for making me a new creation
  that You saw the value of me
Thank You, Lord,
  for teaching me the beauty of holiness
Thank You, Lord,
  that in You I am seated in high places
Thank You, Lord,
  for Heaven's view
Thank you, Lord, Thank You, Lord

— —

**And hope does not disappoint us, because
God has poured out His love into our hearts
through the Holy Spirit, whom He has given us.**

Romans 5:5 BSB

If not for You, Lord,
  there would be no beauty for ashes
If not for You, Lord,
  there would be no joy in the morning
If not for You, Lord,
  there would not be a garment of praise for
  the spirit of heaviness
If not for You, Lord,
  hope would not live
If not for You, Lord,
  love would not conquer all
If not for You, Lord,
  I could not get back up when I fall
If not for You, Lord,
  deliverance could not be mine
If not for You, Lord,
  there would be no find in the loss
If not for You, Lord, If not for You

— �֍ —

**He replied, "Whether he is a sinner or not, I don't know.
One thing I do know. I was blind but now I see!"**

John 9:25 NIV

Thank You, Lord,
   for beauty in the daily
Thank You, Lord,
   that morning-by-morning new mercies I see
Thank You, Lord,
   that You are "my glory, and the lifter
   of my head." (Psalm 3:3 ESV)
Thank You, Lord,
   that You see the good in me
Thank You, Lord,
   for seed for the sower
Thank You, Lord,
   that You have taught me to live
   in the lower
Thank You, Lord,
   that Your grace is always sufficient
Thank You, Lord,
   that life is a forward march
Thank You, Lord, Thank You, Lord

— �֟ —

He must increase, but I *must* decrease.
John 3:30 KJV

If not for You, Lord,
   I would not know that you are my reason
If not for You, Lord,
   my head would hang down
If not for You, Lord,
   I would not know Your presence
   all around
If not for You, Lord,
   my soul would never have been awakened
If not for You, Lord,
   my heart could never have been made new
If not for You, Lord,
   my mind would not have been renewed
If not for You, Lord,
   I would not know Your Holy Spirit
If not for You, Lord, If not for You

— �֍ —

"The LORD your God is among you; He is mighty to save.
He will rejoice over you with gladness;
He will quiet you with His love;
He will rejoice over you with singing."
Zephaniah 3:17 BSB

Thank You, Lord,

   that You make all things beautiful in Your time
Thank You, Lord,

   for a daily view that speaks new
Thank You, Lord,

   that when I seek You, I find You
Thank You, Lord,

   that when I call on You, I find answers
Thank You, Lord,

   for wisdom that cries out
Thank You, Lord,

   for ears that can hear and listen
Thank You, Lord,

   that You never leave me in the dark
Thank You, Lord,

   for being my life's spark that shines brightest
   in the dark
Thank You, Lord, Thank You, Lord

— ✲ —

**For You will light my lamp; The LORD my God
will enlighten my darkness.**

Psalm 18:28 NKJV

If not for You, Lord,

> I would not know your promises are yea
> and amen

If not for You, Lord,

> I would not know that this earth life is not
> the finale

If not for You, Lord,

> I would not know the straight and the narrow,
> I would not know Your word penetrates to
> the marrow

If not for You, Lord,

> I would not know what truly matters

If not for You, Lord,

> I would not know the power of praise

If not for You, Lord,

> I would not know my life could be raised

If not for You, Lord,

> I would not know a friend that sticks closer
> than a brother

If not for You, Lord,

> I would not know that it is You and no other

If not for You, Lord, If not for You

— ✳ —

**You are the God who works wonders; you have made
known your might among the peoples.**

Psalm 77:14 ESV

Thank You, Lord,
> that your promises are true

Thank You, Lord,
> that You make every crooked path straight

Thank you, Lord,
> that You carry me forward

Thank you, Lord,
> that there is nothing you cannot mend
> and restore

Thank You, Lord,
> that my life You have raised

Thank You, Lord,
> that You have taught me how to praise

Thank You, Lord,
> for calling me friend

Thank You, Lord,
> for being with me around all of life's bends

Thank You, Lord,
> that with You eternal life has no end

Thank You, Lord, Thank You, Lord

**Heal me, O LORD, and I shall be healed; save me,
and I shall be saved: for thou *art* my praise.**

Jeremiah 17:14 KJV

If not for You, Lord,

    I would not know the "Wonderful, Counsellor,
    The mighty God, The everlasting Father,
    The Prince of Peace." (Isaiah 9:6 KJV)

If not for You, Lord,

    I would not know the God who is more
    than enough

If not for You, Lord,

    I would not know what to do
    with life's stuff

If not for You, Lord,

    I could not do the tough times

If not for You, Lord,

    I would not know how to climb

If not for You, Lord,

    I would not know that You are always on time

If not for You, Lord, If not for You

He makes my feet like the *feet of* deer,
And sets me on my high places.

Psalm 18:33 NKJV

Thank You, Lord,
    that I can sit in Your lap
Thank You, Lord,
    that I know Your might
    and Your love that holds tight
Thank You, Lord,
    that you never leave me without Your presence
Thank You, Lord,
    that You are my provider
Thank You, Lord,
    that Your yoke is easy, and Your burden is light
Thank You, Lord,
    that Your Word is always bright
Thank You, Lord,
    that my whole life is found in You
Thank You, Lord,
    that You will eternally be my true
Thank You, Lord, Thank You, Lord

For in him we live, and move, and have our being;
as certain also of your own poets have said,
For we are also his offspring.

Acts 17:28 KJV

If not for You, Lord,
> my life messes would not become a message,
> my life tests would not become a testimony

If not for You, Lord,
> I would not know the One who delivers me
> from all my afflictions, who heals all my
> diseases, the One who is touched with the
> feelings of all my infirmities

If not for You, Lord,
> I would not know, for truly wisdom and
> knowledge are found in You

If not for You, Lord,
> I would not know that mercy could rewrite
> my life

If not for You, Lord,
> I would not know that without Your breath I
> would not survive

If not for You, Lord,
> I would not know that with Your sufficient
> grace, I could thrive

If not for You, Lord, If not for You

**Many are the afflictions of the righteous,
but the LORD delivers him out of them all.**

Psalm 34:19 NKJV

Thank You, Lord,
>for giving Your life for mine

Thank You, Lord,
>for being dependable, for being intentional

Thank You, Lord,
>that You had so many reasons to leave and yet You are still here with me

Thank You, Lord,
>that You are faithful and faithful You will always be

Thank You, Lord,
>for being my protector
>from things seen and unseen

Thank You, Lord,
>that Your faithfulness in the past has become hope and confidence for the future

Thank You, Lord,
>that You are always open to conversation, that You said come let us reason together

Thank You, Lord, Thank You, Lord,

The One who calls you is faithful, and He will do it.

1 Thessalonians 5:24 BSB

If not for You, Lord,

I would not know the way I should take,
I would not know the life of beauty You
could make
If not for You, Lord,
I would not know all that You did
was for my sake
If not for You, Lord,
I would not be able to overcome
all of life's aches
If not for You, Lord,
I would not know that silence speaks volumes
If not for You, Lord,
I would not know that prayers are answered
If not for You, Lord,
I would not know that You are fresh air
If not for You, Lord,
I would not know the difference a day
can make
If not for You, Lord, If not for You

— ⚘ —

We love Him, because He first loved us.

1 John 4:19 NKJV

Thank You, Lord,

    that You are the way I should take
Thank You, Lord,

    for making me whole in every part
Thank You, Lord,

    for creating in me a new heart and
    for renewing a right spirit within me
Thank You, Lord,

    for the power of prayer, silent and spoken
Thank You, Lord,

    that you raised me up
    and fathered me as Your daughter
Thank You, Lord,

    that You never sleep nor slumber
    that You are the God who sees
Thank You, Lord,

    that You rose from the tomb and
    that in You there's always room for anyone
    who calls upon Your name
Thank You, Lord, Thank You, Lord

     **And it shall come to pass *That* whoever calls
     on the name of the LORD Shall be saved.**

        Joel 2:32 NKJV

If not for You, Lord,

I would have drowned in the many waters
If not for You, Lord,
the darkness would have consumed me,
I would not have been delivered from my
strong enemy
If not for You, Lord,
I would have no one to teach my hands
to war
If not for You, Lord,
I would have no one to hold me up
If not for You, Lord,
there would be no one to enlighten my darkness
If not for You, Lord,
I would not know what to do in any season
If not for You, Lord,
the path under my feet would not be enlarged
If not for You, Lord,
I would fall and never get back up
If not for You, Lord, If not for You

"For the LORD your God goes with you to fight for you
against your enemies, to give you the victory."

Deuteronomy 20:4 BSB

Thank You, Lord,
> that You uphold all things by the power of Your Word

Thank You, Lord,
> that You are my teacher who teaches me to love God and to love my neighbor

Thank You, Lord,
> that You are light and there is no darkness in You

Thank You, Lord,
> that "You have taken account of my wanderings" and You "put my tears in Your bottle" (Psalm 56:8 BSB)

Thank You, Lord,
> that You lead me by still waters
>
> that You will not allow my foot to slip

Thank You, Lord,
> that when I am down, I am not out, and though I fall, I will rise

Thank You, Lord, Thank You, Lord

**Many waters cannot quench love,
neither can the floods drown it.**

Song of Solomon 8:7 KJV

If not for You, Lord,
    I would not know the cost
If not for You, Lord,
    I would not know I was lost
If not for You, Lord,
    I would not know that the redeemed of the
    Lord can say so
If not for You, Lord,
    I would not know the power of the sow
If not for You, Lord,
    I would not know that I belong,
    I would not know how to be strong
If not for You, Lord,
    I would not know what to do to be forgiven of
    wrongs
If not for You, Lord,
    I would not know I could begin again,
    I would not know that there is an end
If not for You, Lord, If not for You

— ✤ —

Let the redeemed of the LORD say *so*, Whom He
has redeemed from the hand of the enemy,

Psalm 107:2 NKJV

Thank You, Lord,
   that You paid the price for me
Thank You, Lord,
   that You bless me every day
Thank You, Lord,
   that You teach me that you reap what you sow
Thank You, Lord,
   that You keep me in the know
Thank You, Lord,
   for wisdom and knowledge are found in You
Thank You, Lord,
   that I am accepted in the beloved
Thank You, Lord,
   that Your faithfulness endures to all
   generations
Thank You, Lord,
   that You never let me go
Thank You, Lord, Thank You, Lord

— ✣ —

**"Be strong and courageous; do not be afraid or terrified
of them, for it is the LORD your God who goes with you;
He will never leave you nor forsake you."**

Deuteronomy 31:6 BSB

If not for You, Lord,

I would have no one to take me from trial
to triumph, and I would not know that
when I can't You can

If not for You, Lord,

I would not know that I do not have to carry it
by myself

If not for You, Lord,

I would not know that when I worship You,
I start to change into Your image

If not for You, Lord,

I would not know that only Jesus can fill
the holes in my soul, that the garden of
my heart has to be weeded

If not for You, Lord,

I would not know the power of seeds,
I would not know love that stays and
never walks away

If not for You, Lord,

I would not know that rest is proof that
I trust You

If not for You, Lord, If not for You

**"I am the LORD, the God of all mankind.
Is anything too hard for me?
Jeremiah 32:27 NIV**

Thank You, Lord,
 that You always cause me to triumph
Thank You, Lord,
 that You are the strength of my life
Thank You, Lord,
 that You are my portion forever
Thank You, Lord,
 that You are my burden bearer
Thank You, Lord,
 for the freedom I find when I worship You
Thank You, Lord,
 that I can come to You empty and be filled
Thank You, Lord,
 for Your still, small voice that speaks,
 for Your Word that never wavers
Thank You, Lord,
 for teaching me that every choice
 I make in You makes me like You
Thank You, Lord,
 that You cover me with Your feathers and
 under Your wings I find safety
Thank You, Lord, Thank You, Lord!

**"The LORD *is* my portion," says my soul,
"Therefore I hope in Him!"
Lamentations 3:24 NKJV**

If not for You, Lord,
> I could not be healed from the darkest
> of spaces in my journey

If not for You, Lord,
> I would not know that my history is Your story

If not for You, Lord,
> I would not know that I overcome by the blood
> of the Lamb and the word of my testimony

If not for You, Lord,
> I would not know that You have been with me
> all my days

If not for You, Lord,
> I would not know that when my heart is
> overwhelmed You can lead me to the rock
> that is higher than I

If not for You, Lord,
> I would not know that You do not let me go
> I would not know that I can live in the
> solution and not the problem

If not for You, Lord, If not for You

— �֡ —

I will turn darkness into light before them and
rough places into level ground. These things
I will do for them, and I will not forsake them.

Isaiah 42:16 BSB

Thank You, Lord,
    that my times are in Your hands
Thank You, Lord,
    that for my life You have a plan
Thank You, Lord,
    that my purpose is found in You
Thank You, Lord,
    that You remain the same regardless of
    how quickly the world is changing
Thank You, Lord,
    that You are still writing my story
Thank You, Lord,
    for teaching me that prayer not only
    changes things but changes me
Thank You, Lord,
    that You are the God who hears me
Thank You, Lord,
    for showing me that when life gets too hard
    to stand, I can kneel in Your presence and
    be raised up again
Thank You, Lord, Thank You, Lord!

— ✤ —

"For I know the plans I have for you," declares
the LORD, "plans to prosper you and not to
harm you, plans to give you hope and a future."
Jeremiah 29:11 NIV

If not for You, Lord,
>   I would not know that I can trust God with all of it

If not for You, Lord,
>   I would not know that I can trust your timing

If not for You, Lord,
>   I would not know Your leading

If not for You, Lord,
>   I would not know the beauty of coming before You with thanksgiving

If not for You, Lord,
>   I would not know the beauty of laying across my bed and communing with my own heart

If not for You, Lord,
>   I would not know the power of letting go and surrendering all of me

If not for You, Lord,
>   I would not know that I can come to You weary and burdened, and You will give me rest

If not for You, Lord, If not for You

— ✤ —

"Come to Me, all who are weary and burdened, and I will give you rest."
Matthew 11:28 NASB

Thank You, Lord,
>that You are my confidence
>and my chief reward

Thank You, Lord,
>that You have taught me to fight with the
>sword of Your Word

Thank You, Lord,
>that You are the Most High God and Lord
>over all

Thank You, Lord,
>for teaching me to give thanks in all things

Thank You, Lord,
>for showing me how to rejoice, and again,
>I say, rejoice

Thank You, Lord,
>for showing me how to surrender
>and make You my life's choice

Thank You, Lord,
>for saving my soul, for the beauty of knowing
>I can always reach for You

Thank You, Lord, Thank You, Lord

**In every thing give thanks: for this is the
will of God in Christ Jesus concerning you.**

1 Thessalonians 5:18 KJV

If not for You, Lord,

> I would not know the power of gratitude, the power of forgiveness

If not for You, Lord,

> I would not know that "Surely goodness and mercy will follow me all the days of my life."
> (Psalm 23:6 BSB)

If not for You, Lord,

> I would not know that because of my surrender to You, I will dwell in the house of the Lord forever

If not for You, Lord,

> I would not know that "The prayer of a righteous person is powerful and effective."
> (James 5:16 NIV)

If not for You, Lord,

> I would not know love that endures forever, and I would not know unconditional love

If not for You, Lord,

> I would not know that love came down to rescue me

If not for You, Lord, If not for You

**The LORD says, "I will rescue those who love me.
I will protect those who trust in my name."**

Psalm 91:14 NLT

Thank You, Lord,
> that You daily load me with benefits

Thank You, Lord,
> that You have shown me and taught me that love conquers all

Thank You, Lord,
> for teaching me to forgive as Christ has forgiven me

Thank You, Lord,
> for showing me how to live free

Thank You, Lord,
> for teaching me to live a life of honor that speaks You

Thank You, Lord,
> that You declare, "With man this is impossible, but with God all things are possible." (Matthew 19:26 KJV)

Thank You, Lord,
> for showing me that when I lean into You, I will get through to the other side

Thank You, Lord, Thank You, Lord

**"Therefore if the Son makes you free,
you shall be free indeed."**

John 8:36 NKJV

If not for You, Lord,
> I would not know that "A day in your courts is better than a thousand elsewhere."
> (Psalm 84:10 ESV)

If not for You, Lord,
> I would not know that even on the most difficult days You are present

If not for You, Lord,
> I would not know that life does not get better by chance but rather by the choices I make in You

If not for You, Lord,
> I would not know that every day I need to water myself with You

If not for You, Lord,
> I would not know that although my sin was great, Your love was and is greater

If not for You, Lord,
> I would not know that You work while I rest

If not for You, Lord,
> I would not know that the joy of You, Lord, is our strength (Nehemiah 8:10 KJV)

If not for You, Lord, If not for You

I know the LORD is always with me.
I will not be shaken, for he is right beside me.

Psalm 16:8 NLT

Thank You, Lord,

>that You have gone on to prepare a place
>for us

Thank You, Lord,

>that Your name will never lose its power

Thank You, Lord,

>that You are with me every hour

Thank You, Lord,

>for the knowledge of knowing You

Thank You, Lord,

>that You love me with an everlasting love,

>that You have drawn me with everlasting
>lovingkindness

Thank You, Lord,

>for the gift of Your Son sent from above

Thank You, Lord,

>that You "are a shield around me, my glory,
>the One who lifts my head high." (Psalm 3:3 NIV)

Thank You, Lord, Thank You, Lord

**"Yes, I have loved you with an everlasting love;
Therefore with lovingkindness I have drawn you."**

Jeremiah 31:3 NKJV

If not for You, Lord,

    I would not know the power of saying yes

If not for You, Lord,

    I would not know the One who is able to do
    more than I can ask, think, or even imagine

If not for You, Lord,

    I would not know that whatever I am facing
    You can turn it around, that "My times are in
    Your hands." (Psalm 31:15 BSB)

If not for You, Lord,

    I would not know that there is a pace for my
    race, and it is found in You

If not for You, Lord,

    I would not know that You prepare me for
    what is up ahead

If not for You, Lord,

    I would not know the One who "is close to
    the brokenhearted and saves those who are
    crushed in spirit." (Psalm 34:18 NIV)

If not for You, Lord, If not for You

**Now unto him that is able to do exceeding
abundantly above all that we ask or think,
according to the power that worketh in us.**

Ephesians 3:20 KJV

Thank You, Lord,

that You are my yes to Your will and Your way
every day

Thank You, Lord,

for Your love that took me in and changed my
life forever

Thank You, Lord,

for the power of the say in declaring
Your Word

Thank You, Lord,

that You said it is finished and completely done

Thank You, Lord,

that You are the gold in my life's race

Thank You, Lord,

for teaching me the beauty of obedience
being better than sacrifice

Thank You, Lord,

for prayers that availeth much

Thank You, Lord, Thank You, Lord

"For it is not you who are speaking, but *it is* the Spirit of your Father who is speaking in you."

Matthew 10:20 NASB

If not for You, Lord,

I would not know I can trust You with my todays and my tomorrows

If not for You, Lord,

I would not know that You give Your beloved sweet sleep, I would not know a love so deep

If not for You, Lord,

I would not know the blessing of peace

If not for You, Lord,

I would not know that I can hope and praise You all the more

If not for You, Lord,

I would not know that I do not need to lean on my own understanding but rather trust and obey

If not for You, Lord,

I would not know the One who will guide me on the right path

If not for You, Lord, If not for You

— —

I will both lie down in peace, and sleep;
For You alone, O LORD, make me dwell in safety.

Psalm 4:8 NKJV

Thank You, Lord,
    that great is Your faithfulness
Thank You, Lord,
    for Your peace that passes all my understanding
Thank You, Lord,
    that You make all things new
Thank You, Lord,
    that You are fully reliable and completely
    trustworthy
Thank You, Lord,
    that You inhabit the praises of Your people
Thank You, Lord,
    that You put a song in my heart
Thank You, Lord,
    that I can find You, that there is no enemy
    that You can't defeat
Thank You, Lord,
    that You answer prayer
Thank You, Lord, Thank You, Lord

— —

**You *are* my hiding place; You shall preserve me
from trouble; You shall surround me
with songs of deliverance. Selah.**

Psalm 32:7 NKJV

If not for You, Lord,
   I could not believe for the impossible
If not for You, Lord,
   I would not know my Creator and my sustainer
If not for You, Lord,
   I would not know how to fight my battles
   I could be overwhelmed in every season
If not for You, Lord,
   I would not know Jesus, the greatest gift the
   world has ever received, I would not know
   that You sent Your Word to heal me
If not for You, Lord,
   I would not know the One who came to make
   me whole
If not for You, Lord,
   I would not know that faith moves You
If not for You, Lord,
   I would not know that I can be patient and
   stand firm because Your coming is near
If not for You, Lord, If not for You

**You, too, be patient and strengthen your hearts,
because the Lord's coming is near.**
James 5:8 BSB

Thank You, Lord,
    that nothing is impossible to those who believe
Thank You, Lord,
    that You are the gift that keeps on giving
Thank You, Lord,
    that healing is the children's bread, and we
    shall not be denied
Thank You, Lord,
    for Your mercy that fails not
Thank You, Lord,
    that I can rest in Your love
Thank You, Lord,
    that You hold me, and You unfold me
Thank You, Lord,
    that You uphold me with Your righteous right
    hand
Thank You, Lord,
    that You are my Creator and my provider,
    that before I was even formed in the womb
    You knew me
Thank You, Lord, Thank You, Lord

— —

**And my God will supply all your needs according to
His glorious riches in Christ Jesus.
Philippians 4:19 BSB**

If not for You, Lord,

I would not know that I do not need to be conformed to this world but rather transformed by the renewing of my mind

If not for You, Lord,

I would not know that forgiveness is a gift to me from You

If not for You, Lord,

I would not know the beauty of surrendering my will to Yours

If not for You, Lord,

I would not know that I can pray in the spirit at all times

If not for You, Lord,

I would not know that no one keeps their promises like You do

If not for You, Lord,

I would not know that You see me, and You hear me that I am responsible for today, and You hold my tomorrow

If not for You, Lord, If not for You

**Humble yourselves in the sight of the Lord,
and he shall lift you up.**

James 4:10 KJV

Thank You, Lord,
> that when I forgive and release others You forgive and release me

Thank You, Lord,
> for Your Holy Spirit that teaches me to pray

Thank You, Lord,
> that "In Your presence *is* fullness of joy; At Your right hand *are* pleasures forevermore."
> (Psalm 16:11 NKJV)

Thank You, Lord,
> that You are the God who sees me

Thank You, Lord,
> for the family of God

Thank You, Lord,
> that I can encourage myself in You and rehearse Your promises

Thank You, Lord,
> that "Faith is the substance of things hoped for, the evidence of things not seen."
> (Hebrews 11:1 KJV)

Thank You, Lord, Thank You, Lord

— �֭ —

So Hagar gave this name to the LORD who had spoken to her: "You are the God who sees me," for she said, "Here I have seen the One who sees me!"

Genesis 16:13 BSB

If not for You, Lord,
    I would not know that victory is found in You
If not for You, Lord,
    I would not know that my blessed assurance
    is Jesus being mine
If not for You, Lord,
    I would not know that I can trust You
    by day and by night
If not for You, Lord,
    I would not know that when I am stressing
    about something I can put it in Your hands
If not for You, Lord,
    I would not know that You loved me
    even while I was a sinner
If not for You, Lord,
    I would not know the One who will never fail
    nor forsake me
If not for You, Lord,
    I would not know that You fight for me,
    and You have a plan
If not for You, Lord, If not for You

— �֍ —

"The LORD will fight for you; you need only to be still."

Exodus 14:14 BSB

Thank You, Lord,
>that You are the well that will never run dry

Thank You, Lord,
>that You have chosen me,
>and my answer will always be yes

Thank You, Lord,
>that I never have to guess what your promises
>are, for they are yay and amen

Thank You, Lord,
>that in You there is no lack

Thank You, Lord,
>that You are always for me and never
>against me

Thank You, Lord,
>that You have called me to sit
>in heavenly places with You

Thank You, Lord,
>that I can seek the Kingdom of God
>above all else

Thank You, Lord, Thank You, Lord

— ✳ —

**The lions may grow weak and hungry, but those who
seek the Lord lack no good thing.**

Psalm 34:10 NIV

If not for You, Lord,

I would be lost and never found

If not for You, Lord,

I would not know that the victory has already been won

If not for You, Lord,

I would not know that You are bigger than any mountain or obstacle that stands in my way

If not for You, Lord,

I would not know that another day

is another gift from God

If not for You, Lord,

I would not know that while the world keeps on changing, You remain the same, and the cross still stands

If not for You, Lord,

I would not know that You love me too much to leave me

If not for You, Lord, If not for You

— ⚘ —

So Jesus answered and said to them,
"Have faith in God."

Mark 11:22 NKJV

Thank You, Lord,
    that You loved me enough to die for me
Thank You, Lord,
    that You are my redeemer,
    You are my healer,
    You are my restorer
Thank You, Lord,
    that You are my wonderful counselor
Thank You, Lord,
    that You are my High Priest
Thank You, Lord,
    that You deliver me from all of my troubles
Thank You, Lord,
    that You are my great comforter
Thank You, Lord,
    that You are my teacher
Thank You, Lord,
    that You are my provider
Thank You, Lord, Thank You, Lord

**And the whole multitude sought to touch Him,
for power went out from Him and healed *them* all.**
Luke 6:19 NKJV

If not for You, Lord,
> I would not know that God is ever present

If not for You, Lord,
> I would not know that I can choose
> faith over fear

If not for You, Lord,
> I would not know grace and mercy

If not for You, Lord,
> I would not know who I am, for truly I cannot
> know who I am until I know who You are

If not for You, Lord,
> I would not know that "I can do all things
> through Christ who gives me strength."
> (Philippians 4:13 BSB)

If not for You, Lord,
> I would not know that problems which
> seem overwhelming are small compared to
> Your greatness

If not for You, Lord,
> I would not know I am precious
> in Your sight

If not for You, Lord, If not for You

God is our refuge and strength,
an ever-present help in times of trouble.
Psalm 46:1 BSB

Thank You, Lord,
    for the beauty of choice
Thank You, Lord,
    that You hear my voice
Thank You, Lord,
    that I can trust You when it feels like
    I cannot trace You
Thank You, Lord,
    that I am because You are
Thank You, Lord,
    that "It is good to wait quietly for the
    salvation of the LORD." (Lamentations 3:26 BSB)
Thank you, Lord,
    that great is Your faithfulness, Lord, unto me
Thank You, Lord,
    that everything I need in this life is found
    in You
Thank You, Lord,
    that when I seek You, I find You
Thank You, Lord, Thank You, Lord

**Be still and know that I *am* God; I will be exalted
among the nations, I will be exalted in the earth!**

Psalm 46:10 NKJV

If not for You, Lord,
  my life would not be
If not for You, Lord,
  the beauty of the journey I could not see
If not for You, Lord,
  I would not know that the greatest gift in my
  life is Your presence
If not for You, Lord,
  I would not know that love tells the truth, and
  You are love and truth
If not for You, Lord,
  I would not know the God who is more
  than enough
If not for You, Lord,
  I would not know that when I seek to do
  Your will in all I do, You show me the path I
  should take
If not for You, Lord,
  I would not know that I need to never leave
  You out of the equation
If not for You, Lord, If not for You

— —

**Let us hold unswervingly to the hope we profess,
for he who promised is faithful.**

Hebrews 10:23 NIV

Thank You, Lord,
> for salvation so full and so free,
> and that You gave Your life for me

Thank You, Lord,
> that You said it is finished,
> that Your power and love are never diminished

Thank You, Lord,
> that my relationship with You is worth
> whatever it takes to develop, and worth
> whatever I need to lay down to build my
> intimacy with life in You

Thank You, Lord,
> that godliness with contentment is a
> discovery I find in You, and it is a great gain

Thank You, Lord,
> that You are the One who has all the
> solutions, sees every detail, and knows and
> sees what I do not and cannot see or know
> from my view

Thank You, Lord, Thank You, Lord

— ✿ —

But even the very hairs of your head are all numbered.
Fear not therefore: ye are of more value
than many sparrows.

Luke 12:7 KJV

If not for You, Lord,

I would not know the beauty of presence over a present

If not for You, Lord,

I would not know that life is unpredictable, but God is faithful

If not for You, Lord,

I would not know that life is hard, but You are good

If not for You, Lord,

I would not know that I can be strong and courageous, for You are with me wherever I go

If not for You, Lord,

I would not know that You keep me from stumbling

If not for You, Lord,

I would not know that prayer really makes a difference and that prayer should be a way of life

If not for You, Lord, If not for You

Until now you have asked nothing in My name.
Ask, and you will receive, that your joy may be full.

John 16:24 NKJV

Thank You, Lord,
> that because of You I understand the value of being present

Thank You, Lord,
> for the life lessons that I am taught by walking with You

Thank You, Lord,
> that You are the difference in me

Thank You, Lord,
> that I can experience Your faithful love every morning

Thank You, Lord,
> that You reveal to me the way I should go because I long for You

Thank You, Lord,
> that You are not limited to one place

Thank You, Lord,
> that "Where the Spirit of the Lord is, there is freedom." (2 Corinthians 3:17 NIV)

Thank You, Lord, Thank You, Lord

— —

I will instruct thee and teach thee in the way which thou shalt go: I will guide thee with mine eye.
Psalm 32:8 KJV

If not for You, Lord,

>I would not know that what You have waiting for me is greater than anything this world has to offer

If not for You, Lord,

>I would not know that You open doors that no man can close

If not for You, Lord,

>I would not know that I can grow in patience

If not for You, Lord,

>I would not know that I need to live
>for the audience of One

If not for You, Lord,

>I would not know that I should always pray and never lose hope

If not for You, Lord,

>I would not know that it is better to take refuge in You than to put our confidence and hope in people

If not for You, Lord, If not for You

— —

**It is better to take refuge in the LORD
than to trust in princes.**

Psalm 118:9 BSB

Thank You, Lord,

for your Words are true: "I am the door: by me if any man enter in, he shall be saved."

(John 10:9 KJV)

Thank You, Lord,

that I can "Be joyful in hope, patient in affliction, faithful in prayer." (Romans 12:12 NIV)

Thank You, Lord,

that "The Lord is good, a stronghold in the day of trouble, And He knows those who take refuge in him." (Nahum 1:7 NASB)

Thank You, Lord,

that "In due time we will reap if we do not grow weary." (Galatians 6:9 NASB)

Thank You, Lord,

that those who guard their mouth protect their life

Thank You, Lord,

that everything I need to live this life is found in You

Thank You, Lord, Thank You, Lord

For He satisfies the longing soul,
And fills the hungry soul with goodness.

Psalm 107:9 NKJV

If not for You, Lord,
>I would not have the Holy Spirit

If not for You, Lord,
>I would not have a helper

If not for You, Lord,
>I would not have a teacher

If not for You, Lord,
>I would not know that You fill me with joy in Your presence

If not for You, Lord,
>I would not know that no heart is too broken for You to mend

If not for You, Lord,
>I would not know that there is no mountain too big for You to move

If not for You, Lord,
>I would not know that there is nothing that You cannot do

If not for You, Lord,
>I would not know that I am loved and valued by You

If not for You, Lord, If not for You

He heals the brokenhearted and binds up their wounds.

Psalm 147:3 ESV

Thank You, Lord,
> that You did not leave us comfortless

Thank You, Lord,
> that You did not leave us helpless

Thank You, Lord,
> that You did not leave us without instruction

Thank You, Lord,
> that I can give You all my pieces, and You
> make me whole

Thank You, Lord,
> for teaching me to walk with You in
> every season

Thank You, Lord,
> for giving me a new wineskin

Thank You, Lord,
> that You did not bring me this far to leave me

Thank You, Lord,
> that I am complete in You

Thank You, Lord, Thank You, Lord

**Being confident of this very thing,
that He who has begun a good work in you
will complete *it* until the day of Jesus Christ;**

Philippians 1:6 NKJV

If not for You, Lord,

    I would not know that You always have a plan

If not for You, Lord,

    I would not know that when I decrease
    You increase

If not for You, Lord,

    I would not know that You are fighting for me

If not for You, Lord,

    I would not know that love conquers all

If not for You, Lord,

    I would not know that loving God looks like
    loving people

If not for You, Lord,

    I would not know that I can trust You in the
    daytime and in the nighttime

If not for You, Lord,

    I would not know that I can wake up each day
    and live a purposeful life

If not for You, Lord, If not for You

**Love bears all things, believes all things,
hopes all things, endures all things.**

1 Corinthians 13:7 ESV

Thank You, Lord,
for Your purpose and Your plan for me
Thank You, Lord,
for my life's purpose is found in You
Thank You, Lord,
that "Those who humble themselves will be exalted." (Matthew 23:12 NIV)
Thank You, Lord,
that God is fighting for me, and I never need to fear
Thank You, Lord,
that love wins
Thank You, Lord,
for choosing to forgive me
Thank You, Lord,
for teaching me to live in the release of others
Thank You, Lord,
that I can speak the truth in love
Thank You, Lord, Thank You, Lord

— �֍ —

As far as the east is from the west, so far has
He removed our transgressions from us.
Psalm 103:12 BSB

If not for You, Lord,

   I would not know the God life

If not for You, Lord,

   I would not know the attitude of gratitude

If not for You, Lord,

   I would not know that Your silence does not
   mean that You are absent

If not for You, Lord,

   I would not know the path for seeking You

If not for You, Lord,

   I would not know that life on the earth is a brief
   period of existence, and then comes eternity

If not for You, Lord,

   I would not know that I can endure hard
   things with the strength and courage to
   move forward

If not for you, Lord,

   I could not go on when I am weary, I would not
   know that you are the One who sustains me

If not for You, Lord, If not for You

For God alone, O my soul, wait in silence,
for my hope is from him.

Psalm 62:5 ESV

Thank You, Lord,
for times of refreshing
Thank You, Lord,
that You have shown me what You require of me
Thank You, Lord,
that You are my dwelling place
Thank You, Lord,
that in lovingkindness You have led the people You have redeemed
Thank You, Lord,
that You always think of me
Thank You, Lord,
that I can hear You in the gentle whisper
Thank You, Lord,
that I am free when I call Your name
Thank You, Lord,
that You got me, and You carry me forward
Thank You, Lord, Thank You, Lord

And after the earthquake a fire, but the LORD
was not in the fire. And after the fire
the sound of a low whisper.

1 Kings 19:12 ESV

If not for You, Lord,
>I would not know that Your timing is perfect

If not for You, Lord,
>I would not know that Your Word does not return void

If not for You, Lord,
>I would not know the power of getting back up, and without You, there would be no me

If not for You, Lord,
>I would not know what to think on, I would not know that I need to take every thought captive

If not for You, Lord,
>I would not know that I can do all things with Your Son, Jesus

If not for You, Lord,
>I would not know that how my story begins is beyond my control and that I play a pivotal role in how it ends

If not for You, Lord, If not for You

— �֍ —

Let us not grow weary in well-doing, for in due time we will reap a harvest if we do not give up.

Galatians 6:9 BSB

Thank You, Lord,
> that You strengthen me in the wait time

Thank You, Lord,
> that You have taught me that those who
> know You keep Your commandments

Thank You, Lord,
> that when I knock You open the door to me

Thank You, Lord,
> that You are always here for me

Thank You, Lord,
> that You "Make Your face to shine on Your
> servant; save me by Your lovingkindness."
> (Psalm 31:16 MEV)

Thank You, Lord,
> for making me whole in every part

Thank You, Lord,
> for giving me life and life abundantly

Thank You, Lord, Thank You, Lord

— ✣ —

**And He said to her, "Daughter, your faith
has made you well. Go in peace, and
be healed of your affliction."**

Mark 5:34 NKJV

If not for You, Lord,
>   I would not know that You are with me on the mountain and in the valley

If not for You, Lord,
>   I would not know that I can pursue You

If not for You, Lord,
>   I would not know that I have full access to You at all times

If not for You, Lord,
>   I would not know that it is my responsibility to put away childish things

If not for You, Lord,
>   I would not know that You have a pace for my race

If not for You, Lord,
>   I would not know the value of spending time alone with God

If not for You, Lord,
>   I would not know that serving others is a tangible way to bless others and glorify God

If not for You, Lord, If not for You

Seek the LORD and his strength,
seek his face continually.

1 Chronicles 16:11 KJV

Thank You, Lord,
>that You made a way for me

Thank You, Lord,
>for Your direction in my life

Thank You, Lord,
>that You never cease to amaze me
>everywhere, every day

Thank You, Lord,
>that You never stop working

Thank You, Lord,
>for the grace to run my life's race

Thank You, Lord,
>for the strength that I find when I choose to
>wait on You

Thank You, Lord,
>that in You I have a Father

Thank You, Lord,
>for Your yes that inspires me every day

Thank You, Lord,
>for being life to me in the day and in the night

Thank You, Lord, Thank You, Lord

For all the promises of God are "Yes" in Christ. And so through Him, our "Amen" is spoken to the glory of God.

2 Corinthians 1:20 BSB

If not for You, Lord,

> I would not know that I am not defined by my
> past, for You have made me a new creation

If not for You, Lord,

> I would always live in hunger and lack

If not for You, Lord,

> I would not know the One who has all
> the answers

If not for You, Lord,

> I would not know to trust you with my
> whole heart and to not lean on my own
> understanding

If not for You, Lord,

> I would not know that in all my ways, when
> I know You, You will make my crooked
> paths straight

If not for You, Lord,

> I would not know the beauty of my heart and
> my flesh singing for joy to the living God!

If not for You, Lord, If not for You

— ✤ —

Let every thing that hath breath praise the LORD.

Praise ye the LORD.

Psalm 150:6 KJV

Thank You, Lord,
> that no matter what I face today, You are
> bigger than my circumstances

Thank You, Lord,
> that in You I can keep going and be brave

Thank You, Lord,
> that You are the way through,
> and You are my only life's choice

Thank You, Lord,
> that I can pray, "Create in me a clean heart
> and renew a right spirit within me."
> (Psalm 51:10 KJV)

Thank You, Lord,
> that I can recognize Your voice

Thank You, Lord,
> that "The Word became flesh and dwelt
> among us." (John 1:14 NKJV)

Thank You, Lord,
> that every day is a new beginning

Thank You, Lord, Thank You, Lord

— ✣ —

**This is the day that the LORD has made;
let us rejoice and be glad in it.**

Psalm 118:24 ESV

If not for You, Lord,
>I would not know the purpose of life, I would not know how to stay out of strife

If not for You, Lord,
>I would not know that I can turn to You at all times

If not for You, Lord,
>I would not know that I can find You in gain and in loss

If not for You, Lord,
>I would not know that prayer is my weapon in life's battlefield

If not for You, Lord,
>I would not know that the quieter I become, the better I can hear You, I would not know that You hear me and You answer

If not for You, Lord,
>I would not know that You are the Lord who heals me

If not for You, Lord, If not for You

'Call to Me, and I will answer you, and show you great and mighty things, which you do not know.'

Jeremiah 33:3 NKJV

Thank You, Lord,
>that You are the reason why I sing

Thank You, Lord,
>that You are the strength of my life

Thank You, Lord,
>that I am not defined by a season because
>seasons change

Thank You, Lord,
>that in all things I am more than a conqueror
>through You, the One who loves me

Thank You, Lord,
>that I can give You all my cares and
>my concerns

Thank You, Lord,
>that You will perfect everything that
>concerns me

Thank You, Lord,
>that You do not allow pain without allowing
>something new to be born

Thank You, Lord, Thank You, Lord

**O sing unto the LORD a new song:
sing unto the LORD, all the earth.**

Psalm 96:1 KJV

If not for You, Lord,
>   I would not know the value of a day

If not for You, Lord,
>   I would not know that You are more
>   than enough

If not for You, Lord,
>   I would not know that forgiveness is never a
>   one-time thing but rather an ongoing lifestyle

If not for You, Lord,
>   I would not know that death is not the end

If not for You, Lord,
>   I would not know how to trust You in the bend

If not for You, Lord,
>   I would not know that You care, and You
>   share, and I am not alone

If not for You, Lord,
>   I would not know that the first-person prayer
>   changes me

If not for You, Lord, If not for You

**And this is that testimony: God has given us eternal life,
and this life is in His Son.**

1 John 5:11 BSB

Thank You, Lord,
    that my strength for each day comes from You
Thank You, Lord,
    that I can pour out my heart to You, for You
    are my refuge
Thank You, Lord,
    that You are "the Lord who exercises
    kindness, justice, and righteousness on
    earth." (Jeremiah 9:24 NIV)
Thank You, Lord,
    for teaching me that I matter
Thank You, Lord,
    that there is no one like my God
Thank You, Lord,
    that You color my world inside the lines of
    Your Word
Thank You, Lord,
    for the Word of God that never changes
Thank You, Lord, Thank You, Lord

— —

But they that wait upon the LORD shall
renew *their* strength; they shall mount up with
wings as eagles; they shall run, and not be weary;
and they shall walk, and not faint.

Isaiah 40:31 KJV

If not for You, Lord,

I would not have You to trust in every life's storm, I would not know that I can follow You in the dark

If not for You, Lord,

I would not know the One who never fails
I would not know that I am the head and not the tail

If not for You, Lord,

I would not know that those who hope in the Lord will have strength renewed daily

If not for You, Lord,

I would not know that this is the day the Lord has made, and I have so many reasons to rejoice and be glad in it

If not for You, Lord,

I would not know the beauty of keeping my eyes upon You, I would not know that all my life You have been faithful, and all my life You have been good

If not for You, Lord, If not for You

Oh, give thanks to the LORD, for *He is* good!
For His mercy *endures* forever.

Psalm 136:1 NKJV

Thank You, Lord,
   that there is an end to this
Thank You, Lord,
   that my redeemer lives
Thank You, Lord,
   that "The grass withers, the flower fades,
   But the word of our God stands forever."
   (Isaiah 40:8 NKJV)
Thank You, Lord,
   that "I can do all things through Christ who
   strengthens me." (Philippians 4:13 NKJV)
Thank You, Lord,
   that the best is yet to come, and I will
   finish strong
Thank You, Lord,
   that You guide me along the best pathway
   for life
Thank You, Lord,
   that hope sustains me in dark times, for You
   are the light that never goes out
Thank You, Lord, Thank You, Lord

The LORD directs the steps of the godly.
He delights in every detail of their lives.

Psalm 37:23 NLT

If not for You, Lord,
　　I would not know the power of prayer,
　　I would not know that You are fresh air
If not for You, Lord,
　　I would not know that the Spirit of the Lord
　　God is upon me
If not for You, Lord,
　　I would not know Your Words are my daily
　　bread and the joy and rejoicing of my heart
If not for You, Lord,
　　I would not know that who I am matters much
　　more than what I do
If not for You, Lord,
　　I would not know that I find peace in
　　surrendering even when it's not easy
If not for You, Lord,
　　I would not know amazing grace, how sweet
　　the sound, that saved a wretch like me
If not for You, Lord, If not for You

**God made Him who knew no sin to be sin
on our behalf, so that in Him we might
become the righteousness of God.**

2 Corinthians 5:21 BSB

Thank You, Lord,

for prayers that have no bounds

Thank You, Lord,

that "Thy words were found, and I did eat them." (Jeremiah 15:16 KJV)

Thank You, Lord,

that there is a life after this, and I am made new in Christ

Thank You, Lord,

that I am clothed with strength and dignity, and I can laugh without fear of the future. (Proverbs 31:25 NLT)

Thank You, Lord,

that you protect me from all kinds of weapons that try to harm me

Thank You, Lord,

that the Holy Spirit lives in me, your breath is in my lungs

Thank You, Lord,

that I am dearly loved and chosen by God!

Thank You, Lord, Thank You, Lord

— �֍ —

The Spirit of God has made me, and the breath of the Almighty gives me life.

Job 33:4 ESV

If not for You, Lord,

    I would not know that all battles are won in prayer

    I would not know that surrendering to God and His Word is the only way to live

If not for You, Lord,

    I would not know that You go before me and will be with me

If not for You, Lord,

    I would not know that I can talk to You about whatever I am facing

If not for You, Lord,

    I would not know Your provision; "The peace of God, which surpasses all understanding, will guard your hearts and minds through Christ Jesus." (Philippians 4:7 NKJV)

If not for You, Lord,

    I would not know that I can keep on going and You will be the strength that I need

If not for You, Lord, If not for You

"The LORD Himself goes before you; He will be with you.
He will never leave you nor forsake you.
Do not be afraid or discouraged."

Deuteronomy 31:8 BSB

Thank You, Lord,

"For You have been my hope, Sovereign LORD,
my confidence since my youth." (Psalm 71:5 NIV)

Thank You, Lord,
for the rest that comes to those who believe

Thank You, Lord,
that You fight for me

Thank You, Lord,
for Your faithfulness that fails not

Thank You, Lord,
that You lead me in the everlasting way

Thank You, Lord,
that You are in my story

Thank You, Lord,
that "You lead me in your truth and teach me,
for you are the God of my salvation; for you I
wait all the day long." (Psalm 25:5 ESV)

Thank You, Lord,
that "The righteous are bold as a lion."
(Proverbs 28:1 KJV)

Thank You, Lord, Thank You, Lord

— ✻ —

I will bless the LORD at all times;
His praise *shall* continually *be* in my mouth.

Psalm 34:1 KJV

If not for You, Lord,
>I would not know that I can live a God story

If not for You, Lord,
>I would not know that my past is a place of
>learning lessons and never a place where I
>should take residence

If not for You, Lord,
>I would not know the beauty of thanking You
>for what I have and trusting You for what
>I need

If not for You, Lord,
>I would not know that I can trust Your character

If not for You, Lord,
>I would not know that I can trust you forever
>for "In the LORD JEHOVAH *is* everlasting
>strength." (Isaiah 26:4 KJV)

If not for You, Lord,
>my hunger would never be satisfied

If not for You, Lord, If not for You

**My help *comes* from the Lord, Who made heaven
and earth. He will not allow your foot to be moved;
He who keeps you will not slumber.**

Psalm 121:2,3 NKJV

Thank You, Lord,
>   for teaching me how to live,
>   for showing me the power of giving

Thank You, Lord,
>   that You are the Bread of Life,
>   that You are living water, and I never have to
>   thirst again

Thank You, Lord,
>   that Christ in me is my only hope of glory

Thank You, Lord,
>   that You are my way maker

Thank You, Lord,
>   that I can praise You as long as I live with
>   songs of joy

Thank You, Lord,
>   that You are my source, and You make
>   streams in the desert

Thank You, Lord,
>   that You are Emmanuel: God with us

Thank You, Lord, Thank You, Lord

— ✤ —

**But he said to me, "My grace is sufficient for you,
for my power is made perfect in weakness."
...For when I am weak, then I am strong.
2 Corinthians 12:9–10 NIV**

If not for You, Lord,

> I would not know that the quality of my
> thinking determines the quality of my life

If not for You, Lord,

> I would not know that what matters most to
> You is my heart

If not for You, Lord,

> I would not know that "Every good and perfect
> gift is from above." (James 1:17 NIV)

If not for You, Lord,

> I would not know that without Your breath,
> I would not survive

If not for You, Lord,

> I would not know that God can heal anything

If not for You, Lord,

> I would not know that "Blessed is the man
> who trusts in the LORD, whose confidence is
> in Him." (Jeremiah 17:7 BSB)

If not for You, Lord, If not for You

And the whole multitude sought to touch Him,
for power went out from Him and healed *them* all.

Luke 6:19 NKJV

Thank You, Lord,
>that Your Word is active and alive

Thank You, Lord,
>that You give me your joy, and You give me
>your strength

Thank You, Lord,
>that You take me through the trials to
>the triumph

Thank You, Lord,
>that I do not have to worry about anything
>but in everything, through prayer and
>thanksgiving, I can let you know what's on
>my mind

Thank You, Lord,
>that as long as I have You, I have enough

Thank You, Lord,
>that the life in front of me is more important
>than the life behind me

Thank You, Lord,
>that You are my protector in all things

Thank You, Lord, Thank You, Lord

**For we are God's handiwork, created in Christ Jesus to do
good works, which God prepared in advance for us to do.**

Ephesians 2:10 NIV

If not for You, Lord,
    my life would have no meaning,
    I would not know my life's purpose
If not for You, Lord,
    I could not thrive in every season
If not for You, Lord,
    my yes would have no meaning
If not for You, Lord,
    I would not know the power of leaning on You
If not for You, Lord,
    I would not know the One who is the answer
    regardless of the question
If not for You, Lord,
    I would not know the glory and the lifter of
    my head
If not for You, Lord,
    I would not know the One who fights for me
If not for You, Lord,
    I would not know the One who is my provider
If not for You, Lord, If not for You

**And it shall come to pass, that before they call, I will
answer; and while they are yet speaking, I will hear.**

Isaiah 65:24 KJV

Thank You, Lord,

> that "My flesh and my heart may fail, but God is the strength of my heart and my portion forever." (Psalm 73:26 ESV)

Thank You, Lord,

> that You will generously supply all I need

Thank You, Lord,

> that "Surely goodness and mercy will follow me all the days of my life, and I will dwell in the house of the LORD forever." (Psalm 23:6 BSB)

Thank You, Lord,

> that I do not need to worry about anything but instead pray about everything

Thank You, Lord,

> that when I look for You wholeheartedly, I find You

Thank You, Lord,

> that hope has a name, and His name is Jesus

Thank You, Lord, Thank You, Lord

To them God has chosen to make known among the Gentiles the glorious riches of this mystery, which is Christ in you, the hope of glory.

Colossians 1:27 BSB

If not for You, Lord,

>   I would not know that nothing in my life is
>   beyond Your power to heal and restore

If not for You, Lord,

>   I would not know that only Jesus can fill the
>   hole in my soul

If not for You, Lord,

>   I would not know that it is only by Your grace
>   that I can endure hard things

If not for You, Lord,

>   I would not know that I do not have to carry it
>   by myself

If not for You, Lord,

>   I would not know that You wait patiently for
>   me to give You my burdens

If not for You, Lord,

>   I would not know that when I can't, God can

If not for You, Lord,

>   I would not know the balm of Gilead

If not for You, Lord,

>   I would not know about being loved with an
>   everlasting love

If not for You, Lord, If not for You

Love never fails.
1 Corinthians 13:8 NIV

Thank You, Lord,
> that You are my source, and You never run out
> of any good thing

Thank You, Lord,
> for the things that You teach me while
> waiting on You

Thank You, Lord,
> that You have never even had one thought of
> rejection toward me

Thank You, Lord,
> that I can always rejoice, always pray, and
> always give thanks

Thank You, Lord,
> that You will "be a refuge for the oppressed, a
> refuge in times of trouble." (Psalm 9:9 KJV)

Thank You, Lord,
> that You cannot lie, that You are always right
> in everything

Thank You, Lord,
> that "The Son of Man did not come to be
> served, but to serve." (Matthew 20:28 NKJV)

Thank You, Lord, Thank You, Lord

And now these three remain: faith, hope and love.
But the greatest of these is love.

1 Corinthians 13:13 NIV

If not for You, Lord,

> I would not know that You do not call the qualified, but You qualify the called

If not for You, Lord,

> I would not know that it is Your voice that needs to be the loudest in my ears

If not for You, Lord,

> I would not be able to look at the years and see Your faithfulness to me in the land of the living

If not for You, Lord,

> I would not know how much my heart affects my sight

If not for You, Lord,

> I would not know that You restore health and heal wounds

If not for You, Lord,

> I would not know that I am safe in the Father's hands and that You protect and guide me

If not for You, Lord, If not for You

— —

Many *are* the afflictions of the righteous,
But the LORD delivers him out of them all.

Psalm 34:19 NKJV

Thank You, Lord,
  for saying yes
Thank You, Lord,
  that I can worship You until my last breath
Thank You, Lord,
  that the righteous person walks in integrity
Thank You, Lord,
  that You are great, and Your name is mighty
  in power
Thank You, Lord,
  that there is no situation hopeless to God
Thank You, Lord,
  that You are with me wherever I go
Thank You, Lord,
  that I can pour out my heart before You, for
  You are a refuge to me
Thank You, Lord,
  that I can give You thanks with a song
Thank You, Lord, Thank You, Lord

The LORD is my strength and my shield; my heart trusts
in Him, and I am helped. Therefore my heart rejoices,
and I give thanks to Him with my song.

Psalm 28:7 BSB

If not for You, Lord,

I would not know that You give me everything necessary to flourish in every season

If not for You, Lord,

I would not know that I can take Your yoke upon me and learn from You, I would not know that Your yoke is easy, and Your burden is light

If not for You, Lord,

I would not know that You are good even when things are bad

I would not know how to live by faith and not by feelings

If not for You, Lord,

I would not know that when I walk with You, I always arrive on time

If not for You, Lord,

I would not know that "You crown the year with Your goodness, and Your paths drip *with* abundance." (Psalm 65:11 NKJV)

If not for You, Lord, If not for You

**His divine power has given us everything we need
for a godly life through our knowledge of him
who called us by his own glory and goodness.**

2 Peter 1:3 NIV

Thank You, Lord,

that You are a witness to every one of my
life's events

Thank You, Lord,

that through You all things were made;
without You nothing was made that has been
made (John 1:3 NIV)

Thank You, Lord,

that I have freedom in You, I have peace in
You, I have hope in You

Thank You, Lord,

that You are my all-sufficient One, I am
seen by You, I am held by You, and I am
made whole

Thank You, Lord,

that I am forgiven

Thank You, Lord,

that we were the people who were not even
a people, and now we are the sons and the
daughters of God!

Thank You, Lord, Thank You, Lord

— —

**Not that we are sufficient of ourselves to think any thing
as of ourselves; but our sufficiency *is* of God;**

2 Corinthians 3:5 KJV

If not for You, Lord,
> I would not know that, "The name of the LORD *is* a strong tower; The righteous run to it and are safe." (Proverbs 18:10 NKJV)

If not for You, Lord,
> I would not know Your truth: "I am the vine and you are the branches.... For apart from Me you can do nothing." (John 15:5 BSB)

If not for You, Lord,
> I would not know that forgiveness is unconditional

If not for You, Lord,
> I would not know the beauty of giving up my will and surrendering to Yours

If not for You, Lord,
> I would not know that You watch over me, and You will not slumber

If not for You, Lord,
> I would not know that life is a space in time to make decisions for eternity

If not for You, Lord, if not for You

The secret of the LORD *is* with those who fear Him, And He will show them His covenant.

(Psalm 25:14 NKJV)

Thank You, Lord,
    that I can run to You and be safe

Thank You, Lord,
    that You are my reason in every season

Thank You, Lord,
    that You keep me and that You are for me

Thank You, Lord,
    that I can, and I will, stay soft and pliable in
    Your hands

Thank You, Lord,
    that "I will bless the LORD at all times."
    (Psalm 34:1 NKJV)

Thank You, Lord,
    for forgiving all my shortcomings and for
    healing all my diseases

Thank You, Lord,
    that "I am fearfully and wonderfully made."
    (Psalm 139:14 BSB)

Thank You, Lord,
    that I will forget none of Your benefits

Thank You, Lord, Thank You, Lord

Heaven and earth will pass away,
but my words will never pass away.

(Matthew 24:35 NIV)

If not for You, Lord,
> I would walk this journey alone,
> I would not know that I am Your own

If not for You, Lord,
> I would not know how to live present, I would not know the beauty of Your presence

If not for You, Lord,
> I would not know that being grateful needs to be my heart's posture

If not for You, Lord,
> I would not know that with You my trouble has an expiration date

If not for You, Lord,
> I would not know that You died for me, and I cannot live without You

If not for You, Lord,
> I would not know that I can hear You in the silence

If not for You, Lord, If not for You

I say to the LORD, "You are my Lord;
apart from you I have no good thing."

Psalm 16:2 NIV

Thank You, Lord,

that You are the reason I sing

Thank You, Lord,

for teaching me the path of surrender

Thank You, Lord,

that "Anxiety weighs down the heart, but a kind word cheers it up."

(Proverbs 12:25 NIV)

Thank You, Lord,

for your living water that becomes a wellspring within me and causes me to never be thirsty again

Thank You, Lord,

that You are my way maker and my heart mender, You take my pieces and make a masterpiece

Thank You, Lord,

that You teach me about You, how You work, and how You move so that I can walk in Your truth until everything within me brings honor to Your name

Thank You, Lord, Thank You, Lord

— ⚘ —

And it shall come to pass that everyone who calls on the name of the LORD shall be saved.

Joel 2:32 ESV

If not for You, Lord,

I would not know that contentment in this life is a discovery found in a relationship with You

If not for You, Lord,

I would not know Your protection from things I do not even see

If not for You, Lord,

I would not know that I am a winner by the nature of God in me

If not for You, Lord,

I would not know that I can believe and trust You even when You are silent

If not for You, Lord,

I would not know that to worry is honoring the wrong authority, and it gives myself to the wrong thoughts

If not for You, Lord,

I would not know how important it is to water me

If not for You, Lord, If not for You

He gives power to the weak, And to *those who have* no might He increases strength.

Isaiah 40:29 NKJV

Thank You, Lord,

   that I can pour out my heart and my praise to You

Thank You, Lord,

   that You are a restoring God!

Thank You, Lord,

   that when the timing is right, You will make things happen

Thank You, Lord,

   that I can, "Be on guard. Stand firm in the faith. Be courageous. Be strong."

   (1 Corinthians 16:13 NLT)

Thank You, Lord,

   that You are concerned with what matters to me, You have not forgotten me

Thank You, Lord,

   that when I stay aware of eternity, it keeps everything in perspective

Thank You, Lord,

   that in You I always have a reason to smile

Thank You, Lord, Thank You, Lord

— ✠ —

Therefore humble yourselves under the mighty hand of God, that He may exalt you in due time,

1 Peter 5:6 NKJV

If not for You, Lord,

> I would not know fullness of joy found only in Your presence and also not know Your peace that passes all my understanding

If not for You, Lord,

> I would not know Your goodness in the land of the living

If not for You, Lord,

> I would not know that I need not ever fear for You are with me

If not for You, Lord,

> I would not know that those who trust in You are surrounded by lovingkindness

If not for You, Lord,

> I would not know that with each new day comes new mercy, grace, and renewed strength

If not for You, Lord,

> I would not know that Your plan is more beautiful than anything I could possibly desire

If not for You, Lord, If not for You

**Many are the plans in a person's heart,
but it is the LORD's purpose that prevails.
Proverbs 19:21 NIV**

Thank You, Lord,

that "Whoever pursues righteousness and unfailing love will find life, righteousness, and honor." (Proverbs 21:21 NLT)

Thank You, Lord,

for the transforming power of Your Word

Thank You, Lord,

that You empathize with every temptation and struggle I face in this life

Thank You, Lord,

that even to my last breath I can give You praise

Thank You, Lord,

that "Thy word have I hid in mine heart, that I might not sin against thee." (Psalm 119:11 KJV)

Thank You, Lord,

that You are faithful, and Your promises are true

Thank You, Lord,

for the eternal hope that I have in You

Thank You, Lord, Thank You, Lord

— —

The world and its desires pass away, but whoever does the will of God lives forever.

1 John 2:17 NIV

If not for You, Lord,

I would not know that a life of love is always going to be challenged

If not for You, Lord,

I would not know that when I make Your Word the roadmap for my life, it narrows my choices

If not for You, Lord,

I would not know that loneliness is a lie, for You have never left my side

If not for You, Lord,

I would not know that I can hold steady on You and know You will see me through

If not for You, Lord,

I would not know that if I am to grow, I must obey, I would not know that to be or not to be is my decision

If not for You, Lord,

I would not know that You are writing my story, and it will be for Your glory

If not for You, Lord, If not for You

— �֍ —

Being confident of this very thing, that he which hath begun a good work in you will perform *it* until the day of Jesus Christ.

Philippians 1:6 KJV

Thank you, Lord,

that I can involve You in all my decisions, and You will crown me with success

Thank You, Lord,

for the story of Ruth, who went from barely surviving to ending up in the family line of Jesus Christ

Thank You, Lord,

for your promise: "Upon this rock I will build my church; and the gates of hell shall not prevail against it."

(Matthew 16:18 KJV)

Thank You, Lord,

that my "Faith might not rest in the wisdom of men but in the power of God."

(1 Corinthians 2:5 ESV)

Thank You, Lord,

that even in a time of disaster, You will watch over the Godly, and they will always have more than enough

Thank You, Lord, Thank You, Lord

— —

For He satisfies the longing soul,
And fills the hungry soul with goodness.

Psalm 107:9 NKJV

If not for You, Lord,

> I would not know truth, I would not know love that endures forever

If not for You, Lord,

> I would not know the freedom that is found where the Spirit of the Lord is

If not for You, Lord,

> I would not know that Your grace is enough

If not for You, Lord,

> I would not know that when I trust You and do not rely on my own understanding, You will guide me on the right paths

If not for You, Lord,

> I would not know that I need not worry about anything and that I should pray about everything

If not for You, Lord,

> I would not know that every day begins a new chapter

If not for You, Lord, If not for You

And we know that God causes all things to work together for good to those who love God, to those who are called according to *His* purpose.

Romans 8:28 NASB

Thank You, Lord,
  that I will surely recover everything
Thank You, Lord,
  that You have created me in Your own image
Thank You, Lord,
  that Your peace guards my heart and my mind
  and surpasses all understanding
Thank You, Lord,
  that I come alive in You
Thank You, Lord,
  that greatness in You is found in serving
Thank You, Lord,
  that "As water reflects the face, so one's life
  reflects the heart." (Proverbs 27:19 NIV)
Thank You, Lord,
  that "The world and its desires pass away, but
  whoever does the will of God lives forever."
  (1 John 2:17 NIV)
Thank You, Lord, Thank You, Lord

— —

I shall not die, but live,
And declare the works of the LORD.

Psalm 118:17 NKJV

If not for You, Lord,

> I would not know that "Faithful is He
> who calls you, and He also will do it."
> (1 Thessalonians 5:24 NASB)

If not for You, Lord,

> I would not know that I am satisfied in You

If not for You, Lord,

> I would not know that every day is a new
> opportunity to change my life

If not for You, Lord,

> I would not know to "Not worry about
> tomorrow, for tomorrow will worry about
> itself. Each day has enough trouble of its
> own." (Matthew 6:34 NIV)

If not for You, Lord,

> I would not know the beauty of staying
> focused on You

If not for You, Lord,

> I would not know the One who promises calm
> in the storm, light in the darkness, healing for
> the broken, and peace for the restless

If not for You, Lord, If not for You

"Have faith in God," Jesus said to them.

Mark 11:22 BSB

Thank You, Lord,
    that with the calling comes the enabling
Thank You, Lord,
    for the power of choice
Thank You, Lord,
    for the new command You gave
    to love one another
Thank You, Lord,
    that you give second chances
Thank You, Lord,
    for Your thoughts towards me are to give me
    hope and a future
Thank You, Lord,
    for the one who is forgiven much, loves much
Thank You, Lord,
    that "Love never fails."
    (1 Corinthians 13:8 NIV)
Thank You, Lord, Thank You, Lord

— ✤ —

**And to know the love of Christ that surpasses knowledge,
that you may be filled with all the fullness of God.**

Ephesians 3:19 ESV

If not for You, Lord,

    I would not know that You are familiar
with disappointment

If not for You, Lord,

    I would not know that You understand
emotions, frustrations, and temptations
because You faced them while You were in
human form on the earth

If not for You, Lord,

    I would not know that fear of the unknown
can attack everyone, but it is Your perfect love
and Your courage that makes the difference

If not for You, Lord,

    I would not know to, "Love your enemies
and pray for those who persecute you."
(Matthew 5:44 NIV)

If not for You, Lord,

    I would not know that "Without faith it is
impossible to please God, because anyone
who approaches Him must believe that
He exists and that He rewards those who
earnestly seek Him." (Hebrews 11:6 BSB)

If not for You, Lord, If not for You

For we walk by faith, not by sight.
(2 Corinthians 5:7 BSB)

Thank You, Lord,

"For we do not have a High Priest who cannot sympathize with our weaknesses, but was in all *points* tempted as *we are, yet* without sin." (Hebrews 4:15 NKJV)

Thank You, Lord,

that "You *are* my God; Early will I seek You; My soul thirsts for You; My flesh longs for You In a dry and thirsty land Where there is no water." (Psalm 63:1 NKJV)

Thank You, Lord,

"Because Your lovingkindness *is* better than life, My lips shall praise You." (Psalm 63:3 NKJV)

Thank You, Lord,

that I can pray while I wait

Thank You, Lord,

for teaching me "A fool vents all his anger, but a wise man holds it back." (Proverbs 29:11 BSB)

Thank You, Lord, Thank You, Lord

— —

I put my hope in Your word.

(Psalm 119:114 BSB)

If not for You, Lord,

I would not know that life is a fight

If not for You, Lord,

I would not know that through the death of Jesus, I am adopted into Your family

If not for You, Lord,

I would not know that You are the way, and I can entrust my life to You

If not for You, Lord,

I would not know that I can strive to live in peace with everyone

If not for You, Lord,

I would not know Your Spirit that leads me on level ground

If not for You, Lord,

I would not know that I can forget the past and see that You are doing a new thing

If not for You, Lord, If not for You

— —

See, I am doing a new thing! Now it springs up; do you not perceive it? I am making a way in the wilderness and streams in the wasteland.

(Isaiah 43:19 NIV)

Thank You, Lord,
that You listen to my prayers, and You respond

Thank You, Lord,
that I can see Your love and Your goodness
even when You say, "No"

Thank You, Lord,
that I am found in the mystery

Thank You, Lord,
that You sent Your only Son into the world
that I might live through Him

Thank You, Lord,
that You give sight to the blind

Thank You, Lord,
for the new commandment You give to love
one another as You have loved us

Thank You, Lord,
that I can trust You completely and not rely
on my own opinions

Thank You, Lord, Thank You, Lord

**"By this everyone will know that you are
My disciples, if you love one another."**

(John 13:35 BSB)

If not for You, Lord,
> I would not know the experience of Your
> faithful love in the morning

If not for You, Lord,
> I would not know that joy comes in
> the morning

If not for You, Lord,
> I would not know that I can be patient and
> trust You with all of it

If not for You, Lord,
> I would not know that "Weeping may endure
> for a night, But joy comes in the morning."
>
> (Psalm 30:5 NKJV)

If not for You, Lord,
> I would not know that I am accepted in
> the beloved

If not for You, Lord,
> I would not know that my latter days will
> be greater

If not for You, Lord, If not for You

— ✼ —

**Every good and perfect gift is from above,
coming down from the Father of the heavenly lights,
who does not change like shifting shadows.**

(James 1:17 NIV)

Thank You, Lord,
  for the power of a transformed life
Thank You, Lord,
  that I can trust in You, reveal to me the way
  I should go because I long for You
Thank You, Lord,
  that I am not alone in any battle
Thank You, Lord,
  that You help me for truly my help comes
  from the Lord
Thank You, Lord,
  that I am always walking within Your sight
Thank You, Lord,
  that Your delays are not denials
Thank You, Lord,
  that nothing about me is a mistake
Thank You, Lord,
  that happiness is a person, and only Jesus
  can satisfy my longing
Thank You, Lord, Thank You, Lord

For He satisfies the longing soul,
And fills the hungry soul with goodness.

(Psalm 107:9 NKJV)

If not for You, Lord,

>I would not know that "You will keep *him* in perfect peace, Whose mind *is* stayed *on You*, Because he trusts in You." (Isaiah 26:3 NKJV)

If not for You, Lord,

>I would not know that I can call on You, and You will answer me

If not for You, Lord,

>I would not know that it is "'Not by might nor by power, but by my Spirit,' says the LORD Almighty." (Zechariah 4:6 NIV)

If not for You, Lord,

>I would not know that "The fear of the Lord is the beginning of wisdom." (Proverbs 9:10 KJV)

If not for You, Lord,

>I would not know that "God is love, and whoever abides in love abides in God, and God abides in him." (1 John 4:16 ESV)

If not for You, Lord, If not for You

— —

'Ah, Lord GOD! Behold, You have made the heavens and the earth by Your great power and outstretched arm. There is nothing too hard for You.'

Jeremiah 32:17 NKJV

Thank You, Lord,

that You never sleep nor slumber

Thank You, Lord,

that You are my light and my salvation

Thank You, Lord,

for opening my eyes to the wonderful things in Your Word I would never have known

Thank You, Lord,

that now I know, "Whoever finds their life will lose it, and whoever loses their life for my sake will find it." (Matthew 10:39 NIV)

Thank You, Lord,

that You have not left or abandoned me and that you do not show favoritism

Thank You, Lord,

that You turn my hurt, anger, and grief into joy, praise, and peace

Thank You, Lord,

that I have peace with God through Jesus

Then Jesus said to his disciples, "Whoever wants to be my disciple must deny themselves and take up their cross and follow me.

(Matthew 16:25 NIV)

A Simple Prayer

If you are at a place in your life where you've heard about the blessings of God, but you aren't sure about Jesus or about your belief in God, you can say a simple prayer like you're talking to a friend. Jesus was sent into this world by God to bring people back into communion with God, who is sometimes called Abba, Father. Scripture teaches us that Jesus gave His life for us so we would be forgiven of all our shortcomings and receive the blessings of an eternal God in this life and the life to come. Talk to Jesus, ask Jesus to reveal Himself to you, and ask Him to come into your life. I believe that's a prayer Jesus would love to answer. He desires your love and desires for you to receive His.

We love Him because He first loved us.

1 John 4:19 NKJV

"For God so loved the world, that he gave
his only begotten Son, that whosoever
believeth in him should not perish,
but have everlasting life."
John 3:16 KJV

Because, if you confess with your mouth
that Jesus is Lord and believe in your heart
that God raised him from the dead,
you will be saved. For, "everyone who calls
on the name of the Lord will be saved."
Romans 10:9, 13 ESV

If Not, Thank You Prayer

I'm thanking You, Lord, for everything You do for me. You never let me down, You're always there right beside me, and You always help me find the right path, the right words, and even the right prayers. If not for You, Lord, I would have no purpose, I would have no life, and I would still be chasing fantasies and vain things that fade away and harm me on my journey. But You, Lord, saved me from all of that. Thank You, Lord. Thank You for shining the light of Your truth on who I really am, the person I am in You, the person full of new life, new vision, new joy, the person full of Your overwhelming, saturating love that never fails.

I have to be honest with You, Lord, even with all the new. Things get hard in this life, but in the hard times, I know there is someone I can run to, someone who loves me all the way, someone who doesn't give up on me, no matter what.

If not for You, Lord, no one would hear my cries, no one would hear my prayers, but You do, and You know all the things that are best for me.

So today, Lord, I need You to be all that You are for me. I'm thanking You, knowing You will make a way, and I'm believing that whatever way You choose for me, it will be a way filled with the abundant life that I may not see right now, but I know You see it, Lord. You see me, You hear me, and I trust in You.

Thank You, Lord, that if not for You, I would not know how great life really is—how big, how deep, how full life is. It doesn't stop; it keeps on going, and it's never ending. You have placed me in Your life, in Your love. It is a complete love that lacks nothing; it is Your love that can make me say:

"The Lord is my shepherd, I shall not want."
Psalm 23:1 KJV

Thank You, Lord; If Not For You

Psalm 23 NKJV

The LORD is my shepherd;
I shall not want. He makes me to lie down
in green pastures;
He leads me beside the still waters.
He restores my soul;
He leads me in the paths of righteousness
For His name's sake.

Yea, though I walk through the valley
of the shadow of death,
I will fear no evil;
For You are with me;
Your rod and Your staff, they comfort me.

You prepare a table before me in the presence
of my enemies;
You anoint my head with oil;
My cup runs over.
Surely goodness and mercy shall follow me
All the days of my life;
And I will [dwell in the house of the Lord
Forever.

About the Creative Associate

Julio Vitolo

Julio Vitolo grew up in the Bronx, NY, not too far from the Yankee Stadium. He graduated from the City College of New York with a degree in Music and Early Childhood Education. As a "corridor teacher" in an innovative Manhattan school setting, he acquired a keen instinct to recognize and develop the unique gifting within each child. Subsequently, he applied his creative, educational instincts to business and successfully helped people imagine, develop, and market their special interests.

Julio gives credit to his early educational roots: "Inspiring and nurturing children has taught me how to identify, 'brand,' and develop something tangible from a seed of an idea to completion."

As an inspired saxophonist and composer, Julio shares his spiritual inclinations through his gift of music. In all his endeavors, he is passionate about touching others with the love of God through Jesus Christ and is instinctively driven to help others reach their full God-given dreams and potential.

Julio works creatively with Gale on making the invisible things become visible, "from a seed of an idea to completion."

By faith we understand that the universe was created by the word of God, so that what is seen was not made out of things that are visible.

Hebrews 11:3 ESV

Julio's Facebook Page: Julio Vee

YouTube: Julio Vitolo

About the Author

Gale Alvarez

Gale Alvarez is the cofounder and copastor of the Love of Jesus Family Church in Orange, New Jersey. The ministry formally began over thirty-six years ago as Gale and her husband, Pastor Jason Alvarez, traveled extensively with evangelists R. W. Schambach, Nicky Cruz, and other vibrant ministries.

With her eye on restoration, Gale also founded the Women of Purpose ministry and the T.O.P. project, Teens of Purpose ministries, at the Love of Jesus Family Church.

Gale's sensitivity and insightful understanding of human frailty have supernaturally equipped her to restore identity, wholeness, and wellness to the lives of the broken. Gale Alvarez is eternally dedicated to meeting the spiritual, material, and emotional needs of all people.

"I lived many a year as a dead woman walking until I met the Creator who makes all things beautiful in His time. When I learned of His love and allowed Him to take me in, everything changed. He told me of His everlasting love. He drew me with lovingkindness and made me aware of how wonderful we are in His eyes.

Thankfully, I am far from perfect. I still go through hard times, but now He is the difference. I know where to run to, how to get there, and most importantly, who to run to. His love never runs out. He makes us new all over again so that we can live life as a brand-new creation made in His glorious image."

—Gale Alvarez

Endorsements

I have been favored to know Pastor Gale Alvarez as a true mother in the body of Christ. She has the keen ability to see, sift through, groom, speak life into, nurture, comfort, and mother all of those around her. Like a gardener, she puts her hands into the dirt of your life, removing all the weeds brought by pain and trauma and, with grace, both plants and waters seeds for them to later blossom into great representatives of the Kingdom. The vulnerability of what is written throughout the pages of this great work is another example of the healing grace that rests upon Pastor Gale Alvarez. It is through her transparency and sensitivity that I have found a place of sanctuary but, more importantly, healing. It is my prayer that you find this work both refreshing and restorative as you see yourself through the words of Pastor Gale.

—Dr. Reginald Charlestin
Macedonia Worship Center
Winston-Salem, North Carolina

Dr. Gale Alvarez is a true example of what it means to love both God and people. Her interactions with others are a testament to her unwavering kindness, compassion, and empathy. Her presence alone makes people hope again, dream again, and desire God even more. Hence, you will find that this book beautifully reflects and showcases her steadfast faith in a dependable God, even in tough times. Dr. Gale wholeheartedly recognizes that hope perseveres solely through Him, making Him our ultimate source of strength. As you read the words in this book, not only will you learn how to bring your worries to God, but you will also see and experience the goodness of God!

                    —Sherri Taylor
                    Love of Jesus Children
                    Ministry Leader

If Not for You Lord is a beautifully written testament to the transformative power of gratitude and the unending love of God. Pastor Gale's words offer comfort, hope, and a reminder that even in the midst of life's trials, we have so much to be thankful for. With an open heart and unwavering trust in God, she invites us to experience the beauty of finding refuge in God's love—a sanctuary for our hearts to rest. I am honored to endorse Pastor Gale's book, knowing that it will bring the same wisdom, love, and grace to others that she has brought to me. It is a must-read for anyone seeking to discover the beauty and wonder of life that can be found in even the most challenging of seasons.

—Tiana Woods
J.D. Candidate, 2023 |
Harvard Law School

Through Gale Alvarez, I have come to know the power of love from firsthand experience. As she has received of the Father's love, Gale freely gives of love with her whole heart, and truly, this is powerful and life-changing!

—Roberta Sieber
Ministry, Life, and Prayer Partner
for over 35 Years

The heart of God has found a beautiful resting place in Gale Alvarez. The simplicity of her "If Not for You, Lord" words speak of her wondrous inner journey that has allowed the Lord to bring His love, truth, and comfort into our lives. If not for you, Gale, so many of us would not have found the love and life of Christ in us, "the hope of glory." Thank you for being just who you are,

—Regina DeBoer
Ministry, Life, and Prayer Partner
for over 35 Years

Pastor Gale Alvarez, cofounder and copastor of Love of Jesus Church in Orange, NJ, is a woman filled with years of experience, wisdom, and the gentle love of God.

—The Reverend Doctor and
Mrs. Enrique Lopez

Gale Alvarez pours out of her very being and her life experience to engage people where they live.

—Valerie J. Fullilove, Writer/Producer
Trinity Park Productions

Pastor Gale is a visionary with integrity and sterling character. From her gentle elegance, but firm, confident voice, flow volumes of wisdom.

—Bettye Blackston
The Women of Purpose Ministry

If you sit more than two minutes with Gale, you will hear the heartbeat of God.

—Reverend Pat Higgins
Restoration Family Church
Hillside, New Jersey

Gale Alvarez is a woman who puts her actions where her intentions are—just amazing.

—Pastor Cassiaus Farrell, Founder
The Love of Jesus Family Church
Patterson, New Jersey

There has never been a time when Pastor Gale hasn't spoken directly to my heart. We are thankful for her compassion, commitment, and dedication to the people of God.

—Bishop Barbara Glanton, Pastor
The Love of Jesus Family Church
Newark, New Jersey

It is evident that Gale has taken the circumstances that life has served her as opportunities to find God and ever press into a greater love and knowledge of the Most High!

—Barry E. Taylor, Founder
Liberty Ministries Inc.

Pastor Gale's Website:
www.GaleAlvarez.com

Pastor Gale's Facebook Pages:
Gale's HeartBeats & Gale Alvarez

YouTube: Gale Alvarez

Gale is available for speaking engagements and can be contacted at: 973-676-4200

With a grateful heart, I extend a special thanks to all those behind the scenes for their prayers, selfless efforts, and countless hours they invested and freely offered to make *If Not for You Lord* a lively hope and reality in the lives of the readers.

And I pray that we would all know the power of God's love. —Gale Alvarez

Gale's Energizing Books of Promise

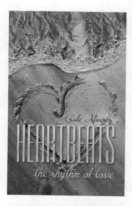

"I am forever changed by His love."
—Gale Alvarez

And God is able to make all grace abound to you, so that in all things, at all times, having all that you need, you will abound in every good work.

2 Corinthians 9:8 BSB

"Fear not, for I *am* with you; Be not dismayed, for I *am* your God. I will strengthen you, Yes, I will help you, I will uphold you with My righteous right hand."

Isaiah 41:10 NKJV

And I pray that you, being rooted and established
in love, may have power, together with all the Lord's
holy people, to grasp how wide and long and high and
deep is the love of Christ, and to know this love that
surpasses knowledge—that you may be filled
to the measure of all the fullness of God.

Ephesians 3:17–20 NIV

So shall My word be that goes forth from My mouth;
It shall not return to Me void, But it shall
accomplish what I please, And it shall
prosper *in the thing* for which I sent it.

Isaiah 55:11 NKJV